RODEO STEER WRESTLING

RODEO

Tex McLeese

The Rourke Press, Inc.
Vero Beach, Florida 32964

PHOTO CREDITS:
© Dennis K. Clark: title page, pages 4, 8, 10, 12, 13, 15, 17, 18, 21; © Texas Department of Tourism: cover; © Pro Rodeo Cowboy Association: page 7

EDITORIAL SERVICES:
Pamela Schroeder

Library of Congress Cataloging-in-Publication Data

McLeese, Tex, 1950-
  Rodeo steer wrestling / Tex McLeese.
    p. cm. — (Rodeo discovery library)
  Includes index.
  ISBN 1-57103-349-1
  1. Steer wrestling. I. Title.

GV1834.45.S73 M34 2000
791.8'4—dc21
                                      00–025071

Printed in the USA

TABLE OF CONTENTS

THE BIG MAN'S EVENT

In **rodeo** (ROW dee oh), steer **wrestling** (REST ling) is sometimes called "the big man's event." A **steer** (STEAR) can weigh more than 500 pounds. Most of the cowboys who try to wrestle a steer weigh about 200 pounds. The steer wrestler is also known as a **bulldogger** (BUHL dawg ur). Smaller cowboys are often rodeo riders or ropers. When you're a bulldogger being big can help you win.

A cowboy attempts
to wrestle a steer.

SIZE ISN'T ENOUGH

No matter how big the cowboy is, the steer will be bigger. In fact, the steer will weigh more than twice as much as a cowboy. This is a sport that calls for skill as well as strength. The cowboy must move the steer in just the right way, so he can use the steer's weight against the animal. The bigger the steer, the harder and faster he can fall.

A steer weighs twice as much as the cowboy.

HISTORY OF STEER WRESTLING

This event began not in the rodeo, but in the **Wild West shows** (WYLD WEST shohz). Unlike rodeos, the shows of William F. "Buffalo Bill" Cody and others were more like plays than sporting events. Performers showed what a cowboy's life was like in the Wild West.

Steer wrestling got its start in the Wild West.

In the 101 Ranch Wild West Show, an African-American cowboy named Bill Pickett showed how to wrestle a steer or a bull to the ground. He learned this skill by watching bulldogs play with the bigger animals. He called his steer wrestling bulldogging. Later, steer wrestling was added between rodeo events. It became an event for cowboys in rodeos.

The wrestler must be careful of the steer's horns.

The hazer and bulldogger trap the steer.

The cowboy leaps from his horse near the steer.

STARTING THE EVENT

The bulldogger and his horse start the event behind a barrier. The steer gets a head start. Then the horse and rider come running after it. If the bulldogger and horse leave too soon, they get 10 seconds added to their time.

The hazer and rider chase down the steer.

THE HAZER

While the bulldogger and his horse chase the steer, another cowboy helps them. This helper is called a **hazer** (I IAY zur). The hazer also rides a horse. It is the hazer's job to keep the steer running in a straight line. Without a hazer's help, the steer could run all over the place. The steer would be a lot harder for the bulldogger to catch. The hazer and his horse are on one side of the steer and the bulldogger and his horse are on the other.

The hazer keeps the steer in line.

WRESTLING THE STEER

When the bulldogger catches up with the steer, he leaps from his horse and grabs the steer by its horns. Then he digs his heels into the dirt and tries to slow the steer down. As he does so, he turns the animal. He lifts up on the right **horn** (HORN) and pushes down on the left horn. He tries to tip the steer over.

Digging his heels in helps slow the steer down.

JUDGING THE EVENT

The bulldogger must stop the steer or change its direction to stop the clock. The steer must be on its side with all four legs pointing the same way. If the steer falls with some of its legs on one side of its body and some on the other, the bulldogger must bring the steer to its feet and try again.

The steer must have all four legs in the same direction.

IS IT DANGEROUS?

It's easy for a cowboy to get hurt when he's wrestling an animal as big as a steer. However, steer wrestling is not the most dangerous rodeo event. Cowboys hurt themselves more often in riding events. They can fall hard from a bull or a bucking bronco. They can get kicked or stepped on by the animal. In fact, one study says that three out of every four rodeo injuries are from riding events. Less than one injury in ten is from steer wrestling. Roping events are the safest of all.

GLOSSARY

bulldogger (BUHL dawg ur) — steer wrestler

hazer (HAY zur) — the steer wrestler's helper, who rides beside the animal to keep it running straight

horn (HORN) — a hard and sharp point sticking out of a steer's head, one by each ear

rodeo (ROW dee oh) — a sport with events using the roping and riding skills that cowboys needed in the Old West

steer (STEAR) — a young ox

Wild West shows (WYLD WEST shohz) — an exhibition or play about the cowboy's life in the Old West; not a competition like a rodeo

wrestling (REST ling) — tipping a steer off its feet and throwing it to the ground

INDEX